dating

younger

women

dating

younger

women

cosmopolitan guide
for the
third millennium

by

kevin doyle

First Doyle Studio Edition 1999

ISBN 0-9652952-7-3

Published in the United States of America by the Doyle Studio Press, Watertown, Massachusetts

CONTENTS

FOREWORD

You will be able to enjoy passionate love affairs
with beautiful younger women in the new
millennium, even if you're not swashbucklingly
handsome. With a little help, a thinking man can
meet and date women in the year 2000 faster
and easier then any other period in history.

All women crave certain qualities in men
which, in a world turning ever more rapidly
toward the mediocre and the commonplace, are
qualities disappearing in the modern single man.
Young women of the future will admire men who
know what they're doing.

There are many types of beautiful women, and
approaching them will always be an exciting and
rewarding experience. Read on and learn how..

dating

younger

women

Chapter I

FRIENDLY ADVICE

YOU SHOULD KNOW

Women are going to be:

Excited about meeting you
Desirous of sex and romance
Appreciative of courtesy
Security-minded
Apt to keep you guessing
More approachable in daylight
Observant of details
Fond of your flaws
Able to see the big picture
Accepting on basis of your behavior

They'll also know better than to:

Use sexual innuendos	Act too eager *
Condescend	Argue
Act indifferent	Assume anything
Give up easily	Compromise dignity

When you approach a girl in the 21st Century....

She'll see you as:	*She'll feel:*
special	flattered
brave	nervous
attractive	hopeful
exciting	self-conscious
sociable	feminine

Chapter II

BASIC TRAINING

GETTING IN SHAPE

So you're going to be slightly north of college
age and, for whatever reason, you think you want
to meet and date Younger Women. Perhaps it's to
gain revenge on your ex-wife, to regain lost youth
or even to prove you're still the same dashing
stud who cut a wide swath through the ladies a
few years previously. Whatever your motives,
you'll have to realize you may be in no condition
to rush into the fray. If you've divorced for less
than three years, your confidence is probably at
an all-time low, and your emotional bankroll
insufficient to withstand rejection.

Take heed, and get into shape, for the joys, vicissitudes and agonies of modern romance.

A WORD TO THE WISE

A word now about the special characteristics of different age groups and, remember, before you start, while young, modern women are definitely what you're going to be after, *you* may not be their idea of Prince Charming. So become strong and healthy. Cast doubt aside. Run, swim, row or do yoga; but **get in shape**. You'll be an experienced man, far more attractive to the opposite sex than will be many of the trendoids and deludinoids they are apt to encounter. To fully adapt your experience and maturity to the millennium dating scene, you must become fit. Dating, like much else in life, will be a game of stamina and nerve. The most successful among us will be those who prevail while expending the least amount of energy.

THE PLAN

The plan (once again if you're going to be past your salad days or recently divorced) will be to warm-up with accessible women of a certain age, **before** working your way down to lyrical beauties of spring.

FOLLOW THESE METHODS

Follow these methods and you'll travel to that magical island in the Sea of Love, where dreams come true and a guy can sail into the sunset, with never a backward glance.

35 TO 39 YEAR OLD WOMEN

If your dating skills are presently less than cutting edge, start first with an ex-housewife. Then work your way through a few swingers, who've drifted into vintage without husbands, before sharpening your corroded wits on independent, self-reliant and career-oriented women. When you're able to successfully to meet, talk and date this last female, then you're ready to move on to a younger age group, closer to the ultimate goal of Younger Woman.

30-34 YEAR OLD WOMEN

Invest some time here, developing and relearning modern postures, outlooks and behaviors. Never underestimate women in this group. They'll be at a point in their lives where they have it all: Looks, experience and strength. Once you've spent time plucking the fruits of this vineyard, you'll be ready to advance to the next group.

25-28 YEAR OLD WOMEN

The twenty-nine year old is omitted from this category because she faces a crisis similar to your own. As she approaches thirty, she'll often be offended by the attention of men her own age or older. In the next millennium, the twenty-nine year old will have become a predator, sometimes prowling unisex gyms and upscale shopping malls looking to reassure and re-establish herself with younger men.

The woman you'll be after, in this phase of your dating development, is the 25 TO 28 YEAR OLD. She'll have retained many attractive qualities of youth, such as an innocent taste in clothes and music, as well as a trusting attitude and sweet desire to love and be loved in return.

You should know the 25 TO 28 YEAR OLD will become possessive more quickly than women in any other age group and you might want to settle here and forsake your journey to the final age group.

20-24 YEAR OLD WOMEN

The sweetest and most appealing of all, she'll crave intimacy more than any other woman. Be anything you want with her and trust her with your deepest feelings. Your most closely held secrets will mean nothing to her, so she'll never use them against you. A relationship with a woman in this age group will always be one of the purest experiences life has to offer.

A word of caution: Remember she'll be growing and developing at a rate ten time faster than you; the relationship may not last and you should let her go, with your blessing, when the time comes.

Travel with her, teach her, cook for her and love her but, when it's time to part, be a man and do the right thing. Let her go and be grateful for the time you've had. Know that you've enriched yourself and become a better person for it.

Chapter III

MEETING THEM

TALK TO THEM

To meet Younger Women, you'll have to talk to them. Compliment an article of their clothing and then make a humorous inquiry. (Like: "How many guys have told you how good you look today?") Never be condescending or obsequious. If you're relaxed and appear slightly indifferent, as though you're the big catch (not her), she'll be more apt to feel comfortable and safe. She'll need to know you're not a threat but, rather, a feather in her cap. Even though her envious girlfriends will eventually offer innocent sounding advice on the impracticality of keeping company with an older man, particularly if their own lives aren't filled with stimulation and joy. Peer acceptance will be important to younger women and we'll discuss later some ways and means to deal with motives spurring a young woman's friends to undermine the pleasure she derives from her relationship with you.

Let's get back to the business of meeting women of the third millennium.

PROJECT SUCCESS

Hold your head high and walk through grand restaurants, extravagant marketplaces and other social splendors, making frequent eye contact, signaling the crowd that you're a man worth knowing. How you present yourself will determine your treatment. If you enjoy interacting with the people you meet, you'll be a hit. Women have always melted in the presence of this kind of confidence.

MONEY

Younger Women will not be as naive as you may want to think and they'll notice the way a man spends his money. If your spending is going to be influenced by ego, this will be seen as weakness by beautiful Younger Women. Don't try to prove your status with your wallet. If you use your money to create an image of yourself, it will be a dead giveaway as to what your values are and, to a certain extent, the content of your character.

BIG CITIES

Big cities will be home to the best and the most beautiful of American women; but the bigger the city, the sharper they are going to be when it comes to reading the motives of a guy like you.

Never break appointments or compromise other relationships to be with a woman. Attaching this kind of undue significance to an encounter will work against you.

SHOPS

No matter what your budget, you can frequent the finest food and clothing stores. Beautiful women are historically accustomed to patronizing the finest of goods and services. Here will be a chance to interact with the niece of the old gentleman selecting that balsamic vinegar from the shelf of a gourmet shop in Pride's Crossing, or an opportunity to nod hello to the dutiful granddaughter at lunch with her forebear in Bronxville.

RESTAURANTS

Trendy coffee shops in posh neighborhoods will always be great places to meet women, especially in the afternoon when beautiful younger women may be relaxing from a shopping spree and receptive to meeting an interesting guy like you.

HOTELS

Lobbies of grand hotels and VIP lounges in international airports are time-honored settings, where you can be sure cupid will continue to fire many an arrow. Sit back, sip the cappuccino, and be prepared to meet beautiful women, as they stream by at all hours of the day and night.

OPENING NIGHT PARTIES

Cultured women will flock opening nights for theatre, ballet, symphony, museum or opera. Check the news for announcements.

RECREATION

Clay courts and dewy links of local country clubs will continue to draw beautiful women, although not to the extent of ski resorts and yacht basins. Sea and snow will have an even more powerful attraction for Millennium's Beautiful Children as they seek to regain innocence and purity through the ocean in summer and the mountains in winter. The best and the most beautiful will always be be found at bistros attracting sailing and ski crowds.

COUNTRY WOMEN

Unless you'll be in a small art town, an authoritative attitude and a big shiny SUV will be the fashion here. Country folk will still crave leadership. A clean shaven few will reign supremely in the sticks and the most attractive men will be the ones who are comfortable in many different situations, particularly when it comes time to venture out and escort country women to any of the wonderful pleasures which can be found only in our major cities.

WHEN YOU'RE AN ARTIST

Beautiful younger women have always been drawn to creative men and artists will have an even more disproportionate need for, and appreciation of, beauty in the future. Certain women will be drawn to the status and stimulation of studio or gallery, so use your special insight to find common ground and treat her to rare observations and visions. Share your insight into the unusual and the incongruous. Spare young Women your unsolicited opinions, while finding and pointing out the beauty or irony of a piece of art, an exotic restaurant, travel destination or personality trait. You'll be giving her the gift of a conversation piece, which she can use later to her own advantage.

ON THE ROAD

If you tend to encounter a bountiful array of waitresses on the road, one way to get acquainted might be to suggest, "how about turning the tables and letting me take you to dinner?". While ON THE ROAD it will be important to strike just the right note of nonchalance. The brief and casual nature of travel will dictate the most laid back approach.

CONFIDENCE

If you want to be as compellingly attractive as you can be, you must feel at ease with others. (A handsome face and an athletic physique, while all well and good, will be no comfort in the many different interpersonal situations we, as human beings, will find ourselves in, over and over again.) You'll be a babe magnet, if you make the most of what you have and learn to really enjoy and appreciate others. If you present yourself to others in an open and confident manner, you'll be far more attractive than the handsome, but arrogant, braggart who's attempting to regale the crowd with boisterous tales of his business prowess.

BELIEVE IN YOURSELF

Believe you deserve the best, and the best will be yours.

Leave behind the naysayers and the underminders. Past mistakes will be history. Make a glorious fresh start. If your name is Percy, you can call yourself Buck. If they're already calling you Butch, you can change your name to Trevor or Humphrey. You can go wherever you like and be what you want; you won't need praise and you'll have no time for criticism. You'll be in full bloom, in total acceptance of yourself and fully able to make the most of your valuable attributes.

Define it any way you want, but your style will be your signature. Louis Armstrong and Cary Grant were both very attractive in their day and in their own way, but they weren't interchangeable. How to find your own style lies within. Be your own man; don't try to be someone else.

The world will always welcome an individualist...

SPEND YOUR TIME AT A WORTHY CAUSE

Whether you're a chess player or a captain of industry, you'll be regarded highly by women if you're highly regarded by your peers. There's no man more attractive to beautiful women then the man who's actually in the arena, the man who, as Teddy Roosevelt put it, "knows the great enthusiasms, the great devotions, who spends himself at a worthy cause."

BE APPRECIATIVE

Once you've achieved health and wealth in the new millennium, it's only natural that you seek the beauty of women; when you understand the meaning of love, beauty, truth and sex, you'll fully appreciate these qualities in your life.

Chapter IV

TALKING TO THEM

MELTING ICE

A humorous question will certainly be an amusing tool for meeting Younger Women. Make up your own quiz. It'll be an effective way of getting to know someone quickly. Put the ball in their court. Women of the 21st Century will be the smartest, strongest and most savvy of all time. There are no correct answers to the questions below, but they can determine a Younger Woman's preferences while MELTING ICE.

"Would you prefer to see a movie staring Leonardo DeCaprio or Anthony Hopkins?"

"Would you rather be tanning in Bermuda or skiing on the slopes of Aspen?"

"Given the choice, would you read a novel by Jane Austen or Danielle Steele?"

"Would you rather see a U2 concert or Paul Simon?"

"Do you consider yourself to be a free spirited adventure seeker or goal oriented decision maker?"

"Do you prefer draft beer or red wine?"

"Who has a more unwavering set of values: Madonna or Hillary Clinton?"

"Do you find yourself ordering more from J. Crew or Victoria's Secret?"

It's important to realize that almost any category can be used when forming these questions as this will be merely a fun way of becoming acquainted. You will be limited only by your imagination and the availability of pen and paper.

Chapter V

DATING

TIPS

Even if you'll have long since gone gray, you'll be
attractive to, and successful with, tomorrow's
woman if you learn to properly answer their most
common inquiries while avoiding manners and
dress certain to turn them off.

Remember this: Even though she's never been
old, she's usually hip to your motives; while you,
who has travelled through youth, will usually be
in the dark as to what's on her mind.

FUTURE TURN-ONS

An expensive haircut
A way with words, as well as an expansive
vocabulary
A clear health consciousness
Rio
Tuxedos
Close shaves
Making it apparent from the start that you are a
man of self-reliance

FUTURE TURN-OFFS

Combed-over bald spots
Poor grammar
Health worries pointing to age
Vegas
Tight or designer Jeans
Beards and mustaches
Any sign of self-pity

BE MATURE

Femmes of the Future will expect, and will be
entitled to, mature emotional behavior from the
men they date.

BE COOL

When you date, don't bombard her with attention
or she might go into a defensive mode. If,
however, she responds to your casual smiles and
comments, accept her interest in you as natural
and deserved. After all, you'll be a good catch,
won't you?

BE ATTENTIVE

Pay attention to her interests. Plan surprises but
don't go overboard in catering to her, or trying to
anticipate her every desire. Be steady..but not too
easy.

ULTIMATUMS

Many people in the brave new world are addicted
to being right and insist on trying to prevail in
every dispute. Never put a relationship on the
line with an ULTIMATUM for a purpose so trite
as winning an argument. There will be
times when losing will be the first step to final
victory.

MAKING IT WORK

A bond between two people will be, at any given time, either strengthening or weakening. A static situation is doomed to boredom and, most likely, dissolution.

LEARN TO COOPERATE

Keep in mind that Tomorrow's Women will have expectations which differ markedly from your own. This could be a breeding ground for self-delusion and can produce a doormat willingness to please on your part. Such a course may lead to disaster. Be true to yourself, to your own needs and beliefs, while understanding that you're both on the same side. It'll be you two against the world. Don't go on the defensive. Offer solutions after every discussion of your differences. Look for opportunities to create commonality.

LEARN TO SHARE

Whenever a man and woman get together, a lot of power will be generated, and that power must be shared in order to keep relationships from disintegrating into futile and debilitating struggles to seize complete control.

LEARN TO STAND UP FOR YOURSELF

Dig your heels in and draw the line when tomorrow's woman tries to see how much she can get away with. Life at the beck and call of another person will be a miserable existence. She'll be secretly pleased with you for standing up to her.

KNOWLEDGE WILL BE POWER

Intelligence will be attractive. Knowledge will be be a powerful force and confidence in that force will lead to a passive man's transformation from nerd to babe magnet. How you harness the POWER OF KNOWLEDGE is up to you.

BE A GENTLEMAN

The attractive passive man will always excuse himself when others begin to engage in crude or ethnic jokes. Women will be drawn to you if you possess an impeccable sense of the appropriate. You should say "thank you" and "pardon me" and never smoke or chew gum in the presence of the Flowers of the Millennium.

LEARN TO LISTEN

With a little couth, the aggressive man will have a devastating effect on tomorrow's driven career women, often sweeping them off their feet and out of their severely cut power suits. Learn to pursue subjects that they find interesting. Listen, pay attention, ask questions; you'll be on your way to success as a social tiger.

BE POSITIVE

Beautiful Young Women will love a big, strong man with a positive attitude who praises the good points in others, both men and women. Always step back when others begin to engage in negativity. You'll be remembered for your understated integrity if you leave a group at the onset of crude or negative chatter.

CHANGE WITH CAUTION

Act to enhance your own style and not to impress anyone else. If you try to change for her sake, instead of your own, be prepared for disappointment. A sudden desire to in-line skate might make her think you're a toady, with less than honorable intentions.
By staying true to yourself, you'll avoid eventual

frustration. This isn't to say you shouldn't defer to her choices eventually, after discussion and with mutual acknowledgment of the compromises involved. It will be only natural to do something for someone you care about.

Chapter VI

SEX WITH TOMORROW'S WOMEN

CANDLELIGHT AND VIOLINS

Beauty will be the greatest aphrodisiac of all.
Never underestimate the advantage of time-
honored seduction tools like candlelight, autumn
foliage, violin music and other pleasures to
which women of any era are entitled.

BE RESPONSIBLE

You'll have a responsibility in any sexual encounter to be honest and open with your partner. Sex is the ultimate opportunity for men and women to work together. You'll owe her every consideration and courtesy for the duration of your relationship.

BE GENEROUS

Don't keep a tally of who's done what for whom in bed. Sex is a mutual act and the exchange of power should flow between the two of you continually and harmoniously. A woman will feel comfortable with a lover who does not judge her, but appreciates her.

LOVE AND SEX

Passionate sex will continue to stimulate wonderful feelings in all of us. Love will take time and trust. It will grow slowly as you get to know each other. Get away together as often as you can, especially if she's under pressure from family and friends to end the relationship or if she's being subject to undue criticism or envy. Younger Women need peer support, perhaps even more than their predecessors, and it's not likely to come from her friends or, for that matter, from cynical or obsolete members of your crowd. New, common interests and friends will be essential to keep the both of you enthusiastic and optimistic, especially after the first flush of passion begins to turn to reality.

Chapter VII

FUTURE SETTINGS

CLUBS

<u>Single Gourmet</u>
133 East 58th Street
New York, NY 10022
(212) 980-8788
Local clubs should be available in about 18 U. S.
cities and Canada; contact local directory
assistance. Will offer dining events with
mingling opportunities, probably mixed with
various outings such as theater, sporting events,
or trips. Current membership (initial, $75,
renewal $40) includes newsletter and reciprocal
membership in all Single Gourmet clubs. Plus
cost of dinner or event.

Parents Without Partners
8807 Colesville Road
Silver Springs, MD 20910
(800) 637-7974
National organization with local chapters around
the country. Will offer activities for single parents
of all ages. Membership fees.

Outdoor Bound
18 Stuyvesant Oval
New York, NY 10009
(212)-505-1020
Outdoors and travel club will offer various trips
with varied activities from rafting to camping.
About ten thousand people on current mailing
list. 1999 membership fee $30.

Chapter VIII

DATING SERVICES

RECOMMENDED

<u>Together</u>
Corporate Office: 161 Worcester Road
Framingham, MA 01701
(508) 620-1115
Matches will be made on basis of questionnaires
and in-depth interviews. Offices likely in 35
U.S. cities, London, and Toronto. Different
membership plans (average annual cost now
about $1,000).

Visual Preference
74 North Maple Avenue
Ridgewood, NJ 07450
(800) 533-1712
Matches will made on basis of video or photo
exchanges.
Will feature glamorous women.

Great Expectations
255 Business Center Drive
Horfam, PA 19044
(215) 957-2780
Offices likely in 50 cities. Choices will be made
by viewing videotapes of clients. Costs about
$1,000 to $2,500 per year.

Conscious Singles Connections
243 West End Avenue, Suite 1504
New York, NY 10023
(212) 873-7187
Matches will be made by member profile through
questionnaire and interview. Will also feature
inspirational tapes, and Meditation for Singles.

Soul Mates
P.O. Box 8691
LoJolla, CA 92038
(619) 259-4321
Matches will be made working one-on-one with a consultant. Relationship skills seminars will be offered offered. Of thousands of clients, a 70 percent success rate is currently claimed.

Field's Exclusive Service
41 East 42nd Street
New York, NY 10017
(212) 391-2233
On the basis of your answers to a questionnaire, this "marriage broker" will provide a list of prospects. Fee will starts at about $50 for three names and depend on the level of service.

Chapter IX

VACATION

RECOMMENDED

<u>Richniks/Perks</u>
362 West 23rd Street
New York, NY 10011
(800) RICHNIK
Social, recreational, and travel opportunities
should abound for Spring/Autumn romance.

Hedonism

Book through travel agents for good prices.
This Jamaica vacation package will continue to be
known for its singles patronage and
uninhibited atmosphere.

Club Med

40 West 57th Street
New York, NY 10019
(800) CLUB MED
All-inclusive vacation packages at villages
around the world offering sports and activities.
Sixty percent of travelers will be single, median
age 35; two-thirds will be professionals.
Membership fee plus cost of trip (week-long,
will be over $1,000).

Chapter X

THE APPROACH

TIPS

Approach in an honest and friendly manner
Do it without hesitation
Act as though she's irresistible
Smile warmly at her
Maintain eye contact
Converse at her pace
Empathize
Keep talk free of pressure
Give her your name
Ask for hers
Offer a handshake during business hours
Offer her a drink or a cup of coffee
Stay focused
Maintain perfect posture
Envision her as a friend for life
Relax and enjoy yourself

GOOD LUCK!

Ruth Leslee Greene

HOW TO
MARRY
MONEY

(PREVIEW FOLLOWS)

*(A taste of Ruth Leslee Greene's
hot new book)*

HOW TO MARRY MONEY

The Simple Path to Love and Glory

RUTH LESLEE GREENE

The Proposition

This book will help you find your pot of gold, but, to live successfully with improved fortune, you will need, as you will see, a heart of gold to match, as well as a certain amount of old-fashioned ruthlessness.

If you believe that one way to a man's heart is through his stomach, this is for you; if you also believe that the way to a man's heart can be the way to the pot of gold at the end of the rainbow, you've got the right book. The examples and instructions herein will show you how to find and marry a rich man.

Study this text and you will be aware of the financial stature of every man in every room you enter. You will recognize many things about his background and pecuniary assets before he even notices the color of your hair. You will know how rich men behave; their likes and dislikes. You will be able to spot phonies. Read this book and you will not only be aware of these things, you'll be able to act on them. You will become objective and systematic.

Prepare, however to bid farewell to the routine. You will be playing a different game. If you resolve to marry money, this book will show how to win the game for keeps.

—R.L.G.

Foreward

There are many types of men with money. Old or young, handsome or hideous, cultured or boorish, sophisticated or callow, elegant or rumpled, intelligent or stupid, all can be found among the rich. It would be a very pleasant task to choose from this list the qualities which you prefer in a rich husband. However, your initial task is not nearly so agreeable. You must first determine the minimum standard or personal qualities in a husband that would be acceptable to you. Can you live with an old, ugly, stupid, vituperative man who is ill-groomed and badly-dressed? If so, you can probably find a rich one who will marry you. But if you require a man who is attractive as well as rich, your chances will be greatly reduced.

Before beginning your quest for a rich husband, you must first determine precisely what grade of man you can attract. If you are fat and illiterate, your options are going to be very limited. But if you can realistically rate yourself as sexy and somewhat genteel, your options are very broad indeed. A self-rating process, however, can be excruciating and never fully accurate. Every one of us has a deep-rooted predisposition toward self-flattery, and one's friends cannot be relied upon for objective perspectives on the quality of one's profile or anything else.

But there is a less tiresome and more precise method for keying yourself to realistic rich targets. Simply reflect for a moment on the sort of men you have been able to attract so far. Has an intelligent, good-hearted, man ever really been interested in you? If so, you will have a reasonable chance with an ugly, intelligent, good-hearted rich man. But you should not anticipate success with a dreamboat, like your former suitor, who in addition happens to be rich. If you would prefer not to spend your life with an ugly man (even a rich one) you can settle for a handsome, intelligent, rich skunk. Do not, however, expect to attract a man who is rich and very desirable to boot.

A functional system for determining the optimum attributes of a rich man with whom you will have a reasonable chance for success is to list the qualifications of the men with whom you have already had genuine intercourse and then delete one of their most endearing qualities and substitute money. To be realistic, you must set your sights lower when you are on the hunt and expect to bag a rich one. This may be disappointing, but it is nonetheless true.

The following advice can give you direction in finding and charming a rich man, but no book can give you the secrets of marrying someone who is an obvious overmatch. No advice can make you significantly more attractive than you already are, and you know instinctively how to use what you have more effectively than anyone can teach you. You are, as Popeye would say, what you are, and you will be recognized as just that. Rich men are not dopes about taking less than they can have; they understand value and are sure to get it.

Believe this final advice, or go out, hunt, find, and fail with a rich nonpareil who has already been pursued by dozens of women more ruthless and probably just as sweet and seductive as yourself. Or use what you will learn in the following pages and go forth to find, tame, and harness a genuine rich man, warts and all!

Although this text addresses the woman's point of view, it works for _men_ by simply reversing genders.

How to Marry Money
The Simple Path to Love & Glory

by Ruth Leslee Greene

This lively book will give you the tools to identify the truly rich. There's new money and there's old money. You may not have a preference, but at least you'll know the difference after reading Ruth Leslee Greene's book.

Where are these people? Where do they play? How do you behave around them? How do you dress? These questions are all answered in this dead-on, yet whimsical, tour of those who are not "asset challenged."

Includes profiles of six people who have achieved true financial security. You'll learn how to pursue the kind of rich person you want to capture as your own.

As Kevin King of Miami says, "Plenty—and I mean plenty— of bangs for your buck. A home run!"

To order, send $12.95 plus $5.00 shipping and handling to:

Doyle Studio Press
294 Pleasant Street
Watertown, MA 02172
Fax 617.926.3156

For MC/VISA/AMEX/Discover orders call 1-888-239-6549 or Fax 1-617-926-3156.

Breakthrough Books

Especially designed for the busy professional man who already gets a lot of women but wants to step up in quality

- **To find the Love of Your Life or simply satisfy the Lust of Your Life**

- **Imparting a special edge to put the thinking man way ahead**

HOW TO ORDER:
- **In the US and Canada: Include $5 for shipping; $8 for 2 or more items.**
- **All other countries: Include $8 for shipping; $16 for 2 or more items.**
- **All international orders must be paid by credit card and will be shipped via airmail.**
- **In the US, payments can also be made by check or money order - sorry, no COD's.**
- **Write quantity and price totals on form.**
- **MC/VISA/AMEX/DISCOVER cardholders may order by phone or fax 24 hours a day.**

FREE BOOK! Order any 4 items and receive a 40-page booklet for picking up women ($12.95 value) absolutely free!

MAIL TO:
Doyle Studio Press
294 Pleasant St.
Watertown, MA 02172

Name _____

Address _____

_____

City _____

State _____ Zip _____

Credit Card # _____

Exp. Date _____

Catalog available

Item #		Title	Price Ea.	Quantity	Total
❏	#001	How to Meet Beautiful Women	$14.95		
❏	#002	Male Sex Machine	$10.95		
❏	#003	Love Magic	$16.00		
❏	#004	How to Marry Money	$12.95		
❏	#005	How to Marry a Beautiful Woman	$9.95		
❏	#006	How to Meet Young Women audio	$23.95		
❏	#007	Beautiful Women audio	$23.95		
❏	#008	Landing the Loaded audio	$23.95		
			Total Merchandise		$
			Shipping (see "HOW TO ORDER")		$
			Total Enclosed		$

Toll free phone: 1-888-239-6549
Fax: 1-617-926-3156
www.meetbeautifulwomen.com